SAVED BY THE BOATS

The Heroic Sea Evacuation of September 11

BY **JULIE GASSMAN**   ILLUSTRATED BY **STEVE MOORS**

Capstone Young Readers
a capstone imprint

An arc of sky framed the city in brilliant blue. The bright, golden sun beamed with warmth. But just below, gray smoke swelled and snaked through the air. And, silently, white ash fell in a thick snowfall, coating the city.

Tragedy was quickly smothering New York City, and its people were searching for a way out. They found their way to the city's edge, held back by the water.

While more than one million people searched for escape, hundreds of boat captains sailed into the destruction. They felt a call to action, a desire to help, a realization that they could provide a safe harbor. They were ordinary people who became heroes on a day when greatness was desperately needed.

A day when the unthinkable had happened.

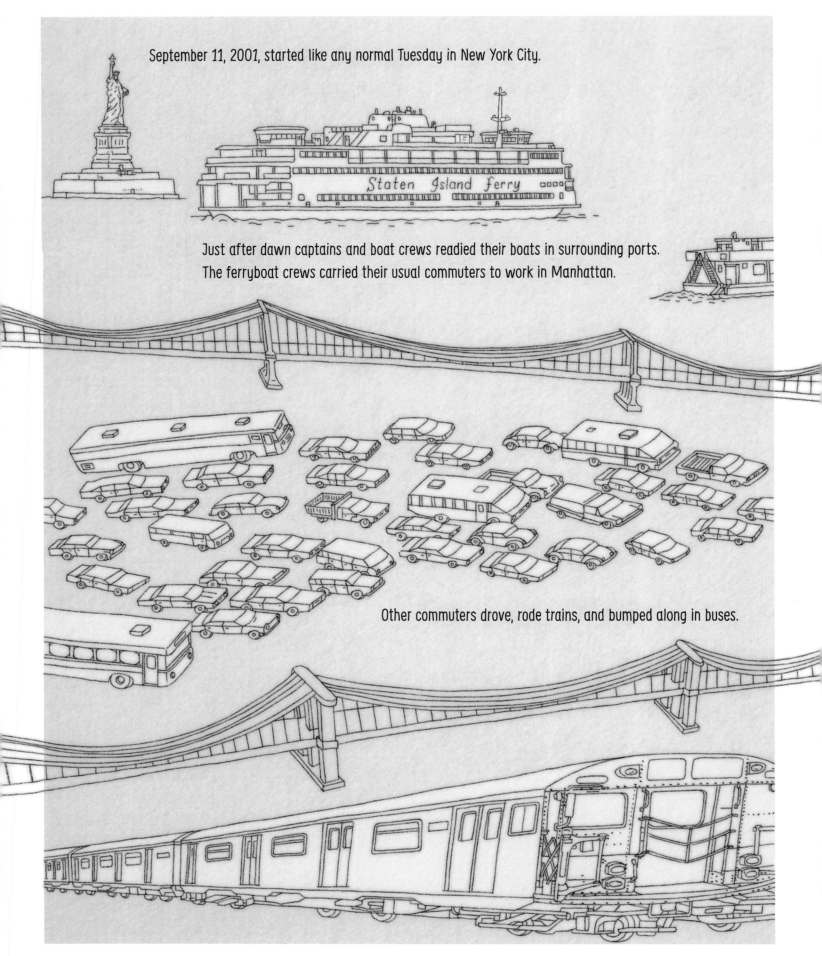

September 11, 2001, started like any normal Tuesday in New York City.

Just after dawn captains and boat crews readied their boats in surrounding ports.
The ferryboat crews carried their usual commuters to work in Manhattan.

Other commuters drove, rode trains, and bumped along in buses.

The city buzzed with activity. Subway riders climbed up the stairs of underground train stations to be greeted by warm sunshine and a cloudless blue sky.

But the beautiful day was soon broken. At 8:46 a.m. an airplane hit one of the city's most recognizable buildings, the World Trade Center's North Tower. At first it seemed as if it were a terrible accident. But when a second airplane hit the South Tower at 9:03 a.m., the message was clear.

New York City—and the United States—was under attack.

That cloudless blue sky was now streaked with gray and black smoke. People desperately tried to flee the scene. Firefighters and police officers rushed to the towers to begin rescue efforts.

New Yorkers from all five boroughs scanned the skies from windows and sidewalks. And boat crews watched the fires rage out of the towers.

But no one expected what came next.

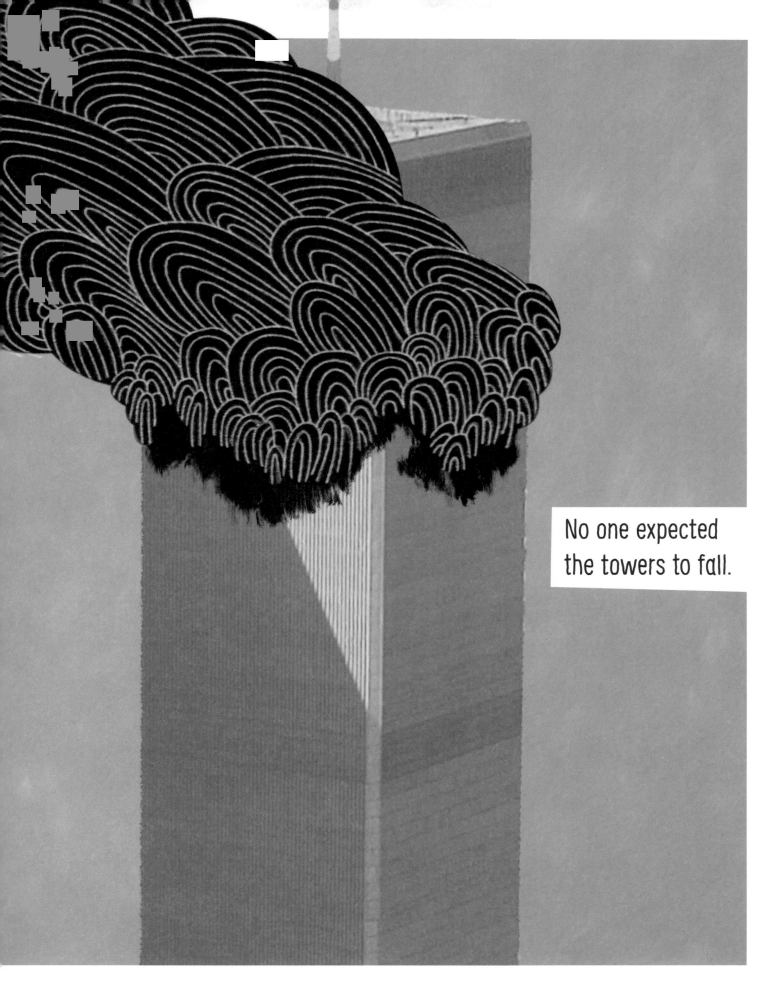

No one expected
the towers to fall.

Suddenly more than one million people were searching for safety. And subways, bridges, and tunnels were closed as a measure of security.

There was only one way off the island—the water.

Fleeing, hundreds of thousands of people ran until they came to the place where the island meets the water. Climbing over railings, they began boarding boats docked in the harbor.

"People were just diving onto the boat," said firefighter Tom Sullivan, who was aboard a fireboat. "We were trying to catch them, trying to help them on. Mothers and nannies with infants in their arms were dropping the children down to us. And then we helped the mothers and nannies down."

Few people stopped to ask where the boats were going.
"These people wanted out of Manhattan ... any way they could," said Captain James Parese.

Coast Guard officials noticed the lines of people growing deeper. Between 11:00 and 11:30 a.m., they put out the call. "All available boats!" rang the marine radios in the harbor and surrounding area. "This is the United States Coast Guard aboard the pilot boat *New York*. Anyone wanting to help with the evacuation of Lower Manhattan, report to Governor's Island."

Boats of all sizes sped into the harbor.

Tugboats, ferryboats, private boats, and party boats.

"If it floated, and it could get there, it got there," said engineer Robin Jones.

And each vessel carried a captain and crew who were ready to serve.

The scene the brave men and women sailed into was grim. The Twin Towers, the tallest buildings in New York City, had stood 110 stories tall. They were replaced with smoke and rubble. The smoke and dust in the air made visibility difficult. Crews knew that boats out on the open water could be easy targets.

But the captains didn't turn around. Instead, they sailed on.

"... that day my biggest concern was the safety of the passengers, the vessel, and my crew and making the right decisions at the right time," explained Captain Parese.

When the captains and crews reached the slips, they saw just how badly they were needed. Many of the people looking for rescue had come from Ground Zero, where the towers once stood. Covered with ash and soot, they carried the weight of the day's tragedy right on their bodies. The crewmates gave towels to these victims, many of whom were crying and shaking with shock.

As one captain later said, "We thought if we could wash some soot off their faces, off their hands ... we could make them more comfortable. We wanted to make them feel that somebody [cared] about what they had just ... gone through."

With loaded boats, captains made their way across the Hudson River. Many of the vessels sailed to Jersey City, New Jersey. There, ambulances with flashing lights waited for injured patients.

The captains knew, too, that people who were displaced from their lower Manhattan homes might find places to stay in Jersey City. Not only did they want to remove people from New York City, they also wanted to help people reach safe destinations.

Meanwhile, back in Manhattan, hours were passing. All along the edge of the Hudson River, lines formed for ferries. Commuters had to walk miles to reach the end of a line.

Police officers warned the wait could be four, five, six hours long. But what choice did the people have but to wait? The police and all who were waiting hoped the crowds would remain calm.

One woman said, "When we arrived at the pier, thousands of people were waiting in line, thousands. Yet, you could hear a pin drop. That was the scariest part about it."

New York City, the city that never sleeps, had become almost eerily calm and quiet.

As time passed, the quiet calm was disturbed by roaring fighter jets. One boat crewmate recalled, "The scariest part was when fighter jets were flying over Manhattan. We didn't know whose they were, and they were coming close to us."

Those waiting in line for evacuation worried too. More than one person asked, "Those are ours, right? Those are American planes?"

And they were.

U.S. military jets were the only planes being allowed to fly in the country's airspace.

The lines moved faster than predicted, no doubt helped by the hundreds of boats that answered the Coast Guard's call for help. After just a couple of hours, passengers boarded boats headed for safety. Many boats announced destinations on bedsheets spray-painted with words like WEEHAWKEN or HOBOKEN, small cities across the river.

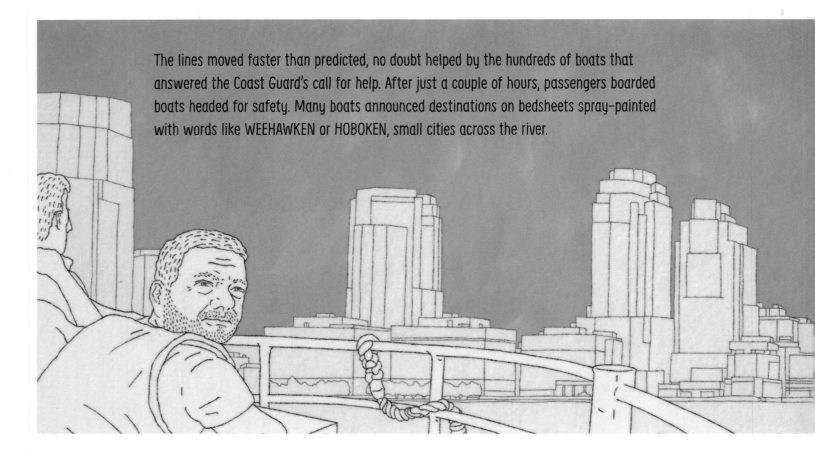

From the ferries, rescued passengers started moving away from the terror of that day. Now they could see the sparkling New Jersey shoreline ahead of them. They were on their way home, or at least out of harm's way.

They had been saved by the boats.

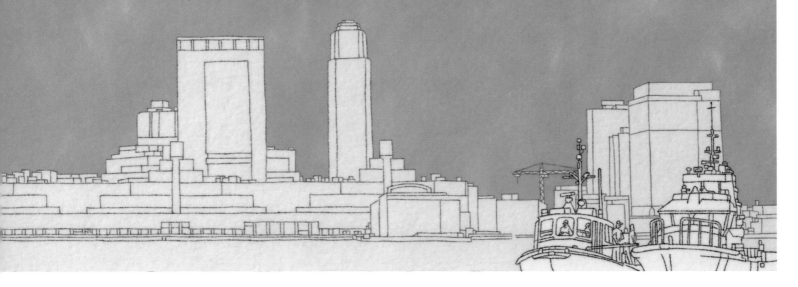

All day long, the boats sailed back and forth, rescuing passengers and then carrying rescue workers, water, and other supplies on their return.

Hundreds of captains and crewmates became heroes that day. Over the course of just nine hours, nearly 500,000 people were evacuated by water.

"It was the greatest thing I ever did with my life," said Captain Rick Thornton.

Engineer Herb Jones described it as "the greatest day that I've ever seen in all ... my life on the water."

It was the largest sea evacuation in history.

It was an answer to a call for help.

It was a light on the city's darkest day.

Author's Note

Like most adults, I have many memories of September 11, 2001, but a few images of the day stand out more vividly than others. My day began like any other workday. After dropping off my infant son at day care, I rode an underground train from Jersey City, New Jersey, into Penn Station in Manhattan.

When I arrived in the city and walked up the subway station stairs into the sunlit September morning, I looked up at the sky. It was a beautiful blue, so striking that I immediately captured it to memory. The blue sky stood out to many New Yorkers that day and is even the inspiration behind an art piece at the National September 11 Memorial Museum.

By the time I reached my office building in Midtown Manhattan, I had heard that a plane had hit one of the World Trade Center towers. And by the time I got to the floor where I worked, I had heard a second plane had hit the other tower. I looked out office windows to see rolling smoke coming from both towers, but the scene of the North Tower smoking and standing alone haunts my memory.

After the subways were shut down, my husband, Nathan, and I decided to walk toward the piers that line the Hudson River to take a boat to New Jersey. As we neared the water's edge, we discovered a huge line of people. We had no other choice but to wait. When the fighter jets flew overhead, another image was captured in my mind.

We waited for under two hours before climbing onto a boat headed for Hoboken, New Jersey. As we rode, I found myself staring at the New Jersey shoreline. Even now it sparkles in my memory, seemingly untouched by the tragedy.

In Hoboken we connected with a friend who gave us a ride first to pick up our son and then take us home. I can still clearly see my baby's face, smiling, happy to see us. I remember feeling grateful that he was too young to know what had happened.

That day, and for many years afterward, I didn't fully realize the enormity of the September 11 boat evacuation. On the tragedy's 10th anniversary, someone sent me a link to the short documentary *Boatlift*. This film helped me understand the importance of the boat evacuation. It introduced me to the heroes who carried victims to safety, workers to their homes, and parents to their children. Now it is with great honor and gratitude that I help share their story, along with illustrator Steve Moors. I, like so many others, am grateful to have been saved by the boats.

Julie Gassman
December 22, 2015

Trying To Remember the Color of the Sky on That September Morning, by Spencer Finch, at the National September 11 Memorial Museum

Glossary

borough—one of the five political divisions of New York City

commuter—someone who travels a long distance to work or school by bus, train, or car

destination—the place to which one is traveling

engineer—the person who operates and maintains a ship

evacuate—to leave a dangerous place to go somewhere safer

evacuation—the removal of large numbers of people leaving an area during a time of danger

Ground Zero—the site in New York City where the Twin Towers of the World Trade Center once stood

pier—a platform that extends over a body of water

port—a harbor where ships dock safely

tragedy—a very sad event

victim—a person who is hurt, killed, or made to suffer because of a disaster, accident, or crime

Thanks to our adviser for her expertise, research, and advice:

Yvonne Simons, Deputy Executive Director
South Street Seaport Museum
New York City, NY

Read More

Aubin, Cheryl Somers. *The Survivor Tree: Inspired by a True Story.* Vienna, Va., 2011.

Benoit, Peter. *September 11 Then and Now.* New York: Children's Press, 2012.

Brown, Don. *America is Under Attack: September 11, 2001: The Day the Towers Fell.* New York: Roaring Brook Press, 2011.

Source Notes

Page 13, line 4: Magee, Mike, editor. *All Available Boats.* New York: Spencer Books, 2002, p. 40:
Page 13, line 9: *Boatlift, An Untold Tale of 9/11 Resilience.* Dir. Eddie Rosenstein. Eyepop Productions, Inc., 2011.
Page 14, line 2: *Boatlift, An Untold Tale of 9/11 Resilience.*
Page 15, line 3: *Boatlift, An Untold Tale of 9/11 Resilience.*
Page 17, line 6: *All Available Boats,* p. 66.
Page 19, line 1: *All Available Boats,* p. 22.
Page 22, line 5: *All Available Boats,* p. 79.
Page 24, line 2: *All Available Boats,* p. 54.
Page 28, line 3: *Boatlift, An Untold Tale of 9/11 Resilience.*
Page 28, line 4: *Boatlift, An Untold Tale of 9/11 Resilience.*

Editor: Shelly Lyons
Designer: Nathan Gassman
Production Specialist: Gene Bentdahl
The illustrations in this book were created digitally.

Encounter is published by Capstone,
1710 Roe Crest Drive, North Mankato, Minnesota 56003
www.mycapstone.com

Library of Congress Cataloging-in-Publication Data
Names: Gassman, Julie, author. | Moors, Steve, illustrator. Title: Saved by the boats : the heroic sea evacuation of September 11 / by Julie Gassman ; illustrated by Steve Moors.
Description: North Mankato, Minnesota : Capstone Press, [2017] Includes bibliographical references.
Identifiers: LCCN 2016001235
ISBN 978-1-5157-0269-6 (library binding : alk. paper)
ISBN 978-1-5157-0270-2 (pbk. : alk. paper)
ISBN 978-1-5157-0275-7 (paper over board : alk. paper)
ISBN 978-1-5157-0271-9 (eBook PDF)
Subjects: LCSH: September 11 Terrorist Attacks, 2001—Juvenile literature. | Evacuation of civilians—New York (State)—New York—Juvenile literature.| Emergency management—New York (State)—New York—Juvenile literature.
Classification: LCC HV6432.7 .G37 2017 | DDC 974.7/1044—dc23
LC record available at http://lccn.loc.gov/2016001235

Image Credit: Newscom/Chris Melzer/dpa/picture-alliance, 31

Printed in China.
022016   009497F16